A Lovely Love Story

for Clare

HarperCollins*Entertainment*
An Imprint of HarperCollins*Publishers*
77–85 Fulham Palace Road,
Hammersmith, London W6 8JB

www.harpercollins.co.uk

Published by HarperCollins*Entertainment* 2004
9

Copyright © Giles Andreae

The Author asserts the moral right to
be identified as the author of this work

A catalogue record for this book
is available from the British Library

ISBN-13   978-0-00-717787-5
ISBN-10   0-00-717787-9

Printed and bound in Italy by L.E.G.O. SpA

All rights reserved. No part of this publication may be
reproduced, stored in a retrieval system, or transmitted,
in any form or by any means, electronic, mechanical,
photocopying, recording or otherwise, without the
prior permission of the publishers.

A LOVELY
LOVE STORY

The fierce Dinosaur was TRAPPED inside his CAGE of ICE.

Although it was COLD he was HAPPY in there. It was, after all, HIS cage.

Then along came the
Lovely Other Dinosaur.

The Lovely Other Dinosaur
MELTED the Dinosaur's
cage with KIND words
and LOVING thoughts.

I LIKE this Dinosaur,
thought the Lovely
Other Dinosaur.

Although he is fierce he
is also TENDER and
he is FUNNY.

He is also quite CLEVER
though I will not tell him
this for now.

I like this Lovely Other Dinosaur, thought the Dinosaur. She is BEAUTIFUL and she is DIFFERENT and she SMELLS so nice.

She is also a FREE SPIRIT which is a quality I much ADMIRE in a dinosaur.

But he can be so DISTANT and so PECULIAR at times, thought the Lovely Other Dinosaur.

He is also overly fond of THINGS.

Are all Dinosaurs so overly fond of THINGS?

But her mind SKIPS from here to there so quickly, thought the Dinosaur. She is also uncommonly keen on SHOPPING.

Are all Lovely Other Dinosaurs so uncommonly keen on shopping?

I will FORGIVE his peculiarity and his concern for THINGS, thought the Lovely Other Dinosaur. For they are Part of what makes him a richly charactered INDIVIDUAL.

I will FORGIVE her SKIPPING MIND and her FONDNESS for shopping, thought the Dinosaur. For she fills our life with BEAUTIFUL thoughts and WONDERFUL Surprises.

Besides, I am not unkeen on SHOPPING either.

Now the Dinosaur and the Lovely Other Dinosaur are OLD.

LOOK at them.

TOGETHER they stand on the hill telling each other STORIES and feeling the WARMTH of the sun on their backs.

And that, my FRIENDS,
is how it is with LOVE.

Let us ALL be Dinosaurs
and Lovely Other Dinosaurs
TOGETHER.

For the Sun is WARM.

And the World is a BEAUTIFUL place.

THE END